# *Green Walks from Oswestry*

### Mary Hignett

## EXPLORING SHROPSHIRE

with
*Shropshire Books*

### Acknowledgements

The publishers would like to thank the Council of the Borough of Oswestry and the Oswestry Ramblers for devising the routes and Harvey Morgan for all his hard work checking, waymarking and repairing the footpaths.

# EXPLORING SHROPSHIRE

*Green Walks from Oswestry* forms part of a series of book and leaflets on walking published by Shropshire Books known as EXPLORING SHROPSHIRE. For other titles in the series see page 38.

Front cover: Oswestry, from the Old Fort, photograph by: Bill Meadows

ISBN: 0-903802-52-X
Text: © Mary Hignett
Cover and book design: Daywell Designs
Illustrations: Kathryn Green
Editing: Helen Sample
Published by Shropshire Books, the publishing division of the Leisure Services department of Shropshire County Council.
Printed in Great Britain by Midland Printing Services.

Supported by the

# Contents

| | |
|---|---|
| Green Walking | v |
| About the Author | vii |
| Key to Maps | ix |
| Old Oswestry Hill Fort | 1 |
| Whittington | 5 |
| Offa's Dyke and Oswestry | 9 |
| Offa's Dyke and Candy Woods | 13 |
| Brogyntyn Hall | 19 |
| Morda Valley | 25 |
| Trefonen | 29 |
| Old Racecourse | 33 |

# Green Walking

Most country walks nowadays require the use of a car to get you to your starting point and to take you home afterwards. The routes in *Green Walks from Oswestry* have been devised for residents and visitors to the town who would like to walk without a car, hence the word 'green' in the title. All the walks start and finish in the town centre, with the exception of one which starts and finishes in the centre of Whittington, a short bus journey away from Oswestry. Each walk takes you out into the surrounding countryside to places of exceptional beauty and interest, and yet still within walking distance of the town.

To help you find your way, the routes have been waymarked where necessary with a special Oswestry sign like the one printed above on this page.

### Rights of Way

Every care has been taken to ensure the accuracy of the maps and route descriptions. The author cannot accept responsibility for misinterpretation by users. If a right of way is obstructed the facts should be reported to Shropshire County Council.

vi

# About the Author

Mary Hignett, a naturalist and keen rambler, was raised in Oswestry and has lived and worked in the area throughout her life.

Her love for and thorough knowledge of the countryside has led her to give much back to the area in her roles as Chairperson of the Montgomeryshire Field Society and the local Border Field Club, and as a member of both the steering committee to form the Shropshire Conservation Trust in 1961, and the Executive Committee of the Council for the Protection of Rural Wales.

An honours degree in geography and geology led to a teaching career as Senior Mistress at Welshpool High School and she was President of Welshpool High School Conservation Club when they won the Prince of Wales Countryside Award in 1970, and the Coca-Cola National Environment Competition in 1973.

Readers of the Oswestry Border Counties Advertizer have been able to share her knowledge down the years through her regular column, and now readers of this book will enjoy her friendly style and fascinating tales of past and present as they walk.

viii

# Key to Map Symbols

| | |
|---|---|
| - - - - - - - | Route of Walk |
| ——————— | Field Boundary |
| ═══════ | Roads |
| ⋯⋯⋯⋯⋯⋯ | Ancient Earthworks |
| —+——+— | Railway |
| ∿∿∿∿ | River or Stream |
| S | Stile |
| G | Gate |
| KG | Kissing Gate |
| S/P | Sign Post |
| WM | Way Marker |
| B FB | Bridge/Foot Bridge |
| P | Parking |
| PH | Public House |
| ♧ | Trees - Deciduous |
| ⋀ | Trees - Coniferous |
| ⬤ | Pond or Lake |
| ♣ | Church with Tower |
| + | R.C. Church |
| ⊻ | Viewpoint |
| ■ | Buildings |
| Ψ | Electricity Pole |

x

# Old Oswestry Fort

OS Map 1:50,000 Sheet No. 126
OS Map 1:25,000 Sheet No. SJ23/33  Distance: 5 miles or 4 miles

*A hilly walk back into history along part of Wat's Dyke and past the ancient hillfort of Old Oswestry.*

1. The walk starts at the Gatacre Playing Fields car park, just behind Woodside School, by a narrow path along its left-hand boundary.

The huge boulder on the car park was dug up during construction work. The only conceivable way such a rock could have been carried from its origin in the Welsh mountains would be embedded in a great ice sheet which moved over the area during the Ice Age. When the ice melted the erratic block was left marooned. Meanwhile great torrents of melt water swept down from the Selattyn area carrying masses of gravel picked up by the ice. When colder spells froze the source of these torrents, their loads were dumped in steep-sided mounds rising up to a hundred feet above the surrounding land. Several such hills are found in this area, the largest and most spectacular being Old Oswestry, with its rings of ramparts, which dominates the view to your right. Another one, locally called "Hill 60" after a first World War battle, rises to the left of the path you are following.

2. The paths leads straight ahead over a stile into a field opposite Old Oswestry. Cross the field to a stile in the corner. Cross the next field to reach another stile. Continue straight ahead and over a stile into hilly pasture. Now climb to the skyline and over a stile into a large open field and make your way down to the far side.

As you walk down, you will see a swampy hollow on your right where curlews nest. Look out for this long-beaked wader whose bubbling song is

Curlew

1

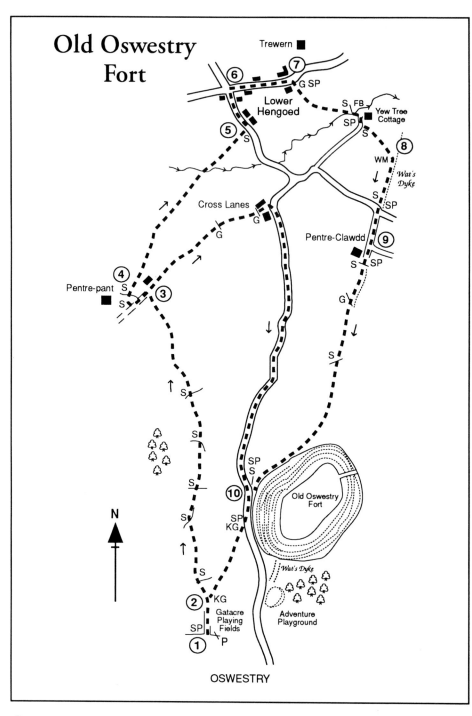

one of the loveliest sounds of the countryside. Here, too, you may see peewits, recognised by their perky crests, for they often feed here in flocks.

3. For the shorter route turn right at the far side of the field along a path which takes you through a series of gates and through Cross Lanes farmyard onto a road. Turn right and continue to the hill fort. Opposite hill fort entrance cross a kissing gate on the other side of the road. Walk diagonally across the fields and through a kissing gate into the narrow path where you started the walk. (2) Retrace your steps to the starting point.

For the longer route turn left at the far side of the field, along the lane to Pentre-Pant until you reach a footpath heading back to the right. Cross the stile in the stone wall and a further stile to take you into a large field.

Pentre-Pant was at one time the residence of John Hamer, Bishop of St. Asaph, who died in 1629 bequeathing money to be divided between the poor of Oswestry and Selattyn parishes.

4. Follow this north-westerly footpath for some distance and across a small stream until it ends at a stile into a narrow lane with some cottages opposite.

5. Turn left in the lane and continue to the crossroads.

6. At the crossroads turn right to Lower Hengoed where the large house, Trewern, is now an old people's home.

7. Where the lane turns sharply left, just past Trewern, rejoin the footpath network on your right by a path which goes through a gate and runs by the hedge, then turns left to the far corner of the field across a stile and sharp right over a stream past Yew Tree Cottage. Head up the track and over the stile immediately on your left to reach Wat's Dyke.

Wat's Dyke, like Offa's Dyke, is thought to have been a boundary dividing the lands of the Celts and Saxons, but it is older than Offa's Dyke. It may originally have been called Watch Dyke from the number of watch-towers along it. Later the land between the two dykes was deemed neutral ground on which trading could take place between the Britons and subsequent invaders.

8. The footpath now turns right to follow Wat's Dyke until a junction of lanes is reached. Follow the smaller lane immediately opposite, and so reach Pentre Clawdd (dyke settlement) a farm on the next corner.

3

9. Your path which is signposted takes you over a stile and by the orchard of the farm, then go through a gate and keeping the hedge on your left head towards the hill fort. The line of trees just to your left marks the continuation of the dyke. Turn right to skirt the foot of the earthworks until a stile is reached into a lane.

Old Oswestry, with its five concentric rings of earthworks, is one of the finest hill forts in Britain, if not in Europe, yet comparatively little is known of its origin. Excavations led by Professor Varley found evidence of early occupation in the Bronze Age, about 550 B.C: Some Roman tiles which suggest they may have sacked it during their occupation and some primitive pottery of the Dark Ages, indicating that it was used again after the Romans left. The lower two ramparts may have been constructed at this time for extra protection.

Locally the earthwork was known as Caer Ogyrfan, and as this was the name of Guinevere's father in the stories of King Arthur it is claimed on rather flimsy evidence that his wife was born here.

10. Now turn left into the lane and about fifty yards further on, right over the kissing gate. Walk diagonally across the field to a second kissing gate (2) and turn left back to the starting point.

The two gravel hills forming Old Oswestry and the adventure playground beyond it were wooded until the 1930s, and so gave the road its name, 'llwyn' meaning wood or grove. They were known locally as the first and second 'coppies' indicating that they were managed by coppicing to supply small timber for the Harlech Estate. Some fine coppiced oaks, with wide boles supporting multiple trunks, can still be seen in the wooded part of the first coppy.

Oswestry Old Fort

# Whittington

O.S.Map 1:50,000 Sheet No. 126   O.S. Map 1:25,000 Sheet No SJ23/33
Starting Point: GR326313   Distance: 8 miles
Bus Service (no.686) every 35 minutes from Oswald Road, Oswestry to Whittington.

*A pleasant walk through pasture and woodland and along part of the Shropshire Union Canal towpath.*

1. The walk starts from the parking area behind Whittington Castle. Turn left along the road, then take the first turn on the right into Top Street. Soon, on your left, is a turn into Daisy Lane which ends at the cemetery car park. Go through the gate to the left of the cemetery and follow the edge of the field.

The old stone gatehouse of the castle fronted by a moat, makes Whittington one of the most picturesque villages of the district. The castle was built in 843 A.D. by a British Chieftain. After the Norman Conquest it became the property of the Peverels and it was given as a dowry to Millet, the progenitor of the line of Fitz Gwarines. One descendant is claimed to have been the squire in whose house Dick Whittington found work after his walk to London, his name having recommended him to the owner.

The castle stood for many centuries but the eastern tower fell in a severe frost in 1960s and some years later much of the western wall was taken down to repair the road to Halston.

The church across the road, originally designed as a chapel for the castle, was rebuilt in brick in the

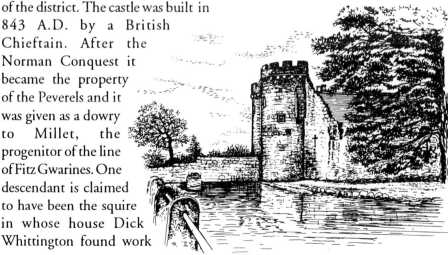

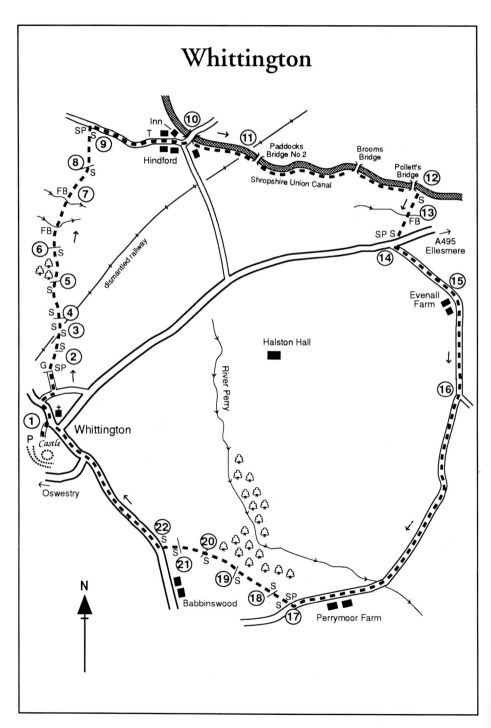

early 19th century, its fifty foot span being supported without pillars. Its best known rector was Reverend, later Bishop, William Walsham How.

2. Cross the stile and keep left.

3. Cross the stile on the left before reaching the corner of the field. Follow the stepped footpath down the bank and cross the line of the old railway. Continue up the far bank and cross the stile at the top.

The old railway track was originally the Cambrian line running from Whittington High Level Station to Whitchurch. For many years after its closure unusual wild flowers could be found along its route, but through time these have been choked out by the more robust grasses of the meadow.

4. Go uphill to the right-hand corner of the field. Cross the stile and continue to follow the field boundary.

5. Cross over the stile just before the woodland and continue along the left side of the field.

6. Cross the stile and continue over the field to cross two footbridges.

7. Continue the line of the path keeping the fence on your right.

8. Cross the stile, then keep left.

This track across the fields is known locally as the miners' road. It is the most direct route to St. Martins. When Ifton Colliery in St Martins was working miners living in Whittington would take this path, which involved a five mile walk, often through soggy ground, before and after a day's work in the pit.

9. Walk past the farm buildings on the left and cross the stile at the far end into a lane. Turn right and in about half a mile you reach the hamlet of Hindford.

10. In the village turn left past Mad Jack's Hotel and, just beyond, go through the wicket gate on your left down to the canal. Turn right along the towpath.

The hotel is named after a well-known local character, Squire Jack Mytton of nearby Halston Hall, who created a legend with his madcap escapades like attempting to jump the toll-gate with a pony and trap. In a short life he squandered a fortune and ended his days in a debtor's prison.

11. Go past the dismantled railway bridge. Continue along the towpath under Paddock Bridge No.2 and Broom's Bridge.

This stretch of the canal is busy in summer time with many long boats cruising from the nearby marina at Maes-y-Termyn, while anglers use these waters frequently, fishing for roach and bream.

12. At the far side of Pollett's Bridge ignore the stile ahead of you and climb up the bank on the right of the canal and cross the stile.

13. Approximately half way down the field, cross to the other side of the hedge to go over a footbridge.

14. Cross the double stile to reach the road, where you turn right, then take the first turn off to the left.

15. Follow the road round to the right after Evenhall Farm.

16. Keep right, ignoring the road off to the left.

17. After Perrymoor Farm, cross the stile on the right.

18. Cross the field and the stile at the far end.

19. Cross the next stile and follow the edge of the wood.

This is part of a woodland which stretches along the River Perry in Halston, once the estate of Jack Mytton. Today herons nest in a northward extension of the wood, so you may be lucky enough to see this large grey wading bird flying over with long legs stretched out behind.

20. Cross the stile, go straight across the field and continue through the gap in the hedge to the next stile.

21. Cross the stile and continue across the next field.

22. Cross the stile on to the main road. Turn right and follow the road back into Whittington.

The hamlet near to where your field track strikes the main road is called Babbinswood. It is often associated with the story of 'The Babes in the Wood', for this is said by some to be based on the murder hereabouts of a five year old child by his uncle in order to obtain his inheritance of £5 a year.

Heron

# Offa's Dyke and Oswestry

O.S. Map 1:50,000 Sheet No 126, O.S. Map 1:25,000 Sheet No SJ22/32
Distance: 7 miles

*A scenic walk through Llanforda park and along part of
Offa's Dyke Path*

1. The walk starts at Castle View where car parking is available. Walk to Bailey Head and continue down Bailey Street to the Cross.

The Bailey Head was originally the outer courtyard of the castle, where justice was dispensed and produce sold. These functions have continued to the present day. The Guildhall houses the magistrates court on the left, and the Powys Hall market beyond.

2. Turn right into Upper Brook Street and continue straight on past the turning to Welsh Walls and Oswald Place. At the forked roads, bear right into Broomhall Lane.

Beyond the new houses on your left, you reach the roadside house of Broomhall Gardens, the last remnant of the home of Oswestry's "Talley Ho V.C.", General Campbell. The General was decorated for the part he played in a charge by the Coldstream Guards when he rallied his men with a hunting horn - hence his nickname.

3. Past the house, cross a stile on your left leading to a field path running under an electricity pylon.

The pylon, like the housing estate, show how modern living has propelled the old picturesque approach to Oswestry into the twentieth century.

4. The path leads to another stile by which you enter the Lower park of Llanforda. Follow path across the field to a gate.

When Llanforda was still occupied by local gentry, carriages were driven through this park to cross Pinfold Lane through two white gates and enter the inner park. Today the carriage drive is barely distinguishable from a cart track to your left, but you should make for this and go through the gate into the lane.

5. Turn left along the lane and in less than a hundred yards turn into a smaller lane on the right, signposted Candy. Continue along the lane for about a mile until you reach a bridge

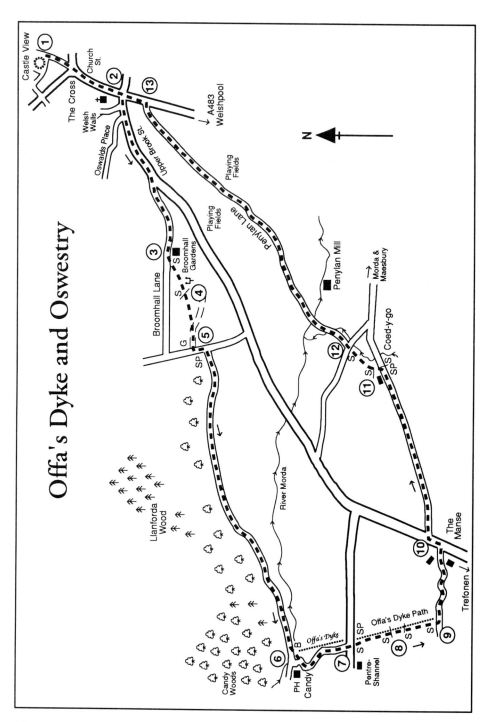

across a stream.

This a warm, sheltered lane where wild flowers abound, particularly on the right, south-facing bank. There are nut trees to start, a patriotic show of red dead nettle, white hedge parsley and blue alkanet where the lane borders Llanforda park, then bluebells and violets in the shade of Candy Woods. Now the lane drops steeply to the bridge which replaces the old ford across the Morda Brook.

**6. Now turn left to pass the Old Mill Inn and follow the lane round a sharp bend and then uphill.**

The Morda, still in its infancy flows swiftly and was used to turn a number of mills in the district. The first, Llanforda Mill, ground corn and was the focus of a cluster of cottages which make up the hamlet of Candy.

The old mill was destroyed by fire, but the Old Mill Inn, an attractive stone building has arisen, phoenix-like from the charred shell. Near the entrance, a pebbled millstone is a reminder of its former use, when a stream gushed out from beneath its walls through a fern-filled trough.

Should you pause for breath near the sharp right bend, it is worth looking back to the wooded escarpment of Candy, particularly in autumn when all the colours of sunset make a spectacular mosaic.

**7. At the main road, cross over to a stile leading to the Offa's Dyke Path just to the left of the old farmstead of Pentre-shannel, and follow the edge of the field.**

As you walk along the crest of the old earthwork, which is the dyke, with the flat plain of Shropshire to your left and the hills of Wales tumbling down towards you on the right, it is easy to fall back in imagination to the time, 1,200 years ago, when the newly made earthwork was a frontier

The Old Mill Inn

between Saxon and Celt. Today the turbulence is forgotten and the silence broken only by the raucous cries from a nearby rookery.

8. The Offa's Dyke Footpath takes you through two more fields where the earthwork becomes less apparent as wear and ploughing have reduced it to the level of the fields.

9. The narrow stile from the third field leads into a lane where you turn left.

Now the way becomes less rural as you pass some old coal working and new houses to reach the main Trefonen road by the Manse.

10. Turn left along the road, then in a hundred yards, right following the road sign to Morda and Maesbury.

Soon now you have evidence of Morda's busy industrial past, firstly in the row of attractively modernised cottages, which were originally built as shops for the miners in the Coed-y-go Pit. A little further along comes the white-walled former pub then two cottages adapted from the pit's offices.

11. Cross the stile by the side of the cottages and continue along the path by the hedge. Cross a stile into the next field and cross diagonally to the right, then alongside a small stream.

In the second field a number of unnatural seeming mounds are the spoil heaps of the old pit, reclaimed now by nature into grassy hillocks.

12. Leave the field by a stile into a lane. Cross over this and continue down Penylan Lane which is immediately opposite.

The lane drops steeply down a shady bank, bordered by violets and wood anemones in the spring, until it reaches a little stone bridge across the river Morda. Downstream on your right a tall chimney marks the site of Pen-y-Llan Mill, the second corn mill turned by this busy stream. The chimney was built to convert to steam power, but so quickly did trade develop in the late 18th century that cheap imported grain made the mill redundant before the conversion was complete.

After the parkland of Pen-y-Llan, the scene becomes more urban, first passing between the school playing fields of Oswestry School and The Marches and then into the town. The wide field on your left, behind the Scout Hut was the scene of the great battle of 642 when King Oswald, who is remembered in the name of the town, was slain.

13. Where the lane meets the main road to Welshpool, turn left into Upper Church Street and return to Castle View.

# Offa's Dyke and Candy Woods

O.S. Map 1:50,000 Sheet No.126, O.S. Map 1:25,000 Sheet No SJ 22/32
Distance: 8 miles or 7½ miles

*A varied walk along part of Offa's Dyke, through ancient woodlands and back through parkland.*

1. The walk starts at Castle View where car parking is available. Walk to the Bailey Head and continue down Bailey Street to the Cross. Then follow Church Street to the traffic lights.

At the end of Bailey Street, the fine restored timbered building, probably dating back to the 14th century known as Llwyd Mansion, belonged to the Lloyds of Llanforda, ardent royalists and keen gardeners of the 17th century.

Part way down Church Street, on your left, is the site of New Gate, one of the entrances to the walled town until the late 18th century. The site is now marked by one of the pillars, where the toll for bringing in merchandise was collected. The original gate had a white horse cut into the stone over the arch, dated 1570.

Next door but one, the present chemist's shop was previously an inn called The White Horse and the sign, in relief, is still on its facade. During the general election of 1832, Tory fervour turned to a riot in which the horse's front leg was broken off and its knee joint hurled through the window of a leading Liberal. Today, a century and a half later, the horse still prances on three legs.

Further along, the Wynnstay Hotel,

Llwyd Mansion

# Offa's Dyke and Candy Woods

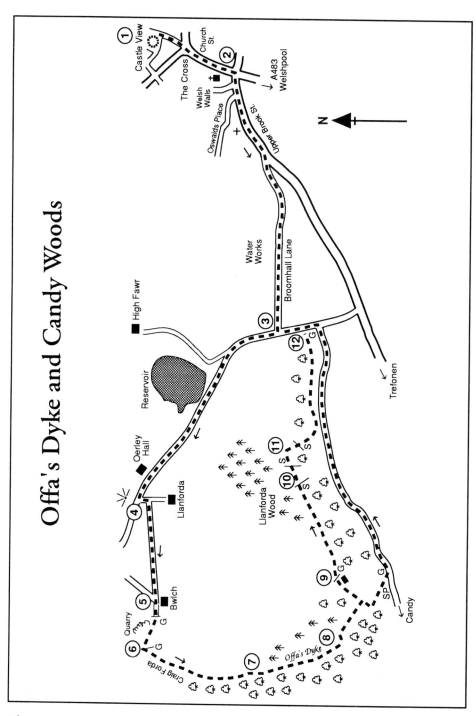

formerly called the Bowling Green and often the Cross Foxes from the coat of arms of the Wynnstay estate, was, until about 1800, just a small public house. Considerable additions and improvements were made when it became a staging post for the coaching traffic along the London to Holyhead highway.

On your right, by the traffic lights, the Coach and Dogs, now a restaurant, was reputedly built about 1600 by Edward Lloyd of Llanforda as an inn to stable the light dog-cart in which he frequently road into town.

**2. Turn right into Upper Brook Street and continue straight on past the turning to Welsh Walls and Oswald's Place to the fork where you will bear right into Broomhall Lane.**

When you have passed the Roman Catholic Church, the broad meadow beyond is the site of the battle in 642 where Oswald, Christian King of Northumbria, was slain by Penda the pagan ruler of Mercia. His head and arms were impaled in Cae'r Groes, the field of the cross, on which Oswestry School now stands. This great British King, by the manner of his death, gave Oswestry its name, and the monastery erected for prayers for his soul was the nucleus of the original 7th century town.

As you take the right fork into Broomhall lane, you go along what was formerly the most attractive entrance to the town, where the trees on either side almost met overhead and their gnarled roots projected like ribs in the steep embankment.

The new housing development on the left stands where previously stood Broom Hall the home of General Campbell V.C., one of two Oswestrians to receive this honour in the first World War. As Lieut-Col. Campbell he was decorated in recognition of the gallant part he played in a charge by the Coldstream Guards, when he rallied his men with a hunting horn. Thereafter he was know affectionately as the "Talley-Ho V.C.".

Just above, on the right, is the tree-lined drive leading to the filter beds where water from Lake Vyrnwy is treated before continuing to Liverpool. This land is a little enclave owned by North-West Water in the midst of the Severn-Trent region.

**3. At the T-junction turn right and follow the main road past the entrance to High Fawr and uphill, along the edge of the reservoir. Llanforda Woods can be seen across the fields to the left.**

The waters from Lake Vyrnwy flow by gravity through pipes across the Morda Valley and under Offa's Dyke, and are first released into the open in the reservoir on your right. This regulating reservoir, which helps to reduce pressure lower down the system is now a gathering ground for water birds where Canada geese and black-headed gulls can always be seen.

**4. When Oerley Hall is reached on your right, turn left into the lane marked Llanforda, which soon turns right into a tree-lined lane.**

As you turn from the main road you have a fine view of the hills of north Montgomeryshire with the Breiddens dominating the foreground, Long Mountain stretching away to the right and Bromlow Callow, Cordon and the Kerry Hills in the background.

**5. When the Bwlch farm is reached the lane again turns sharply right but a farm track runs straight ahead. Follow this track and beyond the gate continue along a cart track with a high bank to the left.**

To the right of the track is an old quarry in which it is possible to find fossils. These are mostly impressions of bi-valves which lived in a shallow sea where sand and grit were being deposited 250 million years ago. These grits, now compressed and solidified, make up the hard rock which forms the Racecourse ridge.

**6. Continue through the gateway where a signpost marks the directions of several footpaths.**

**Follow the path which leads uphill and to the left.**

You are now walking part of the Offa's Dyke long distance path which here runs just below the crest of Craig Forda, a steep escarpment clothed with the mixed deciduous woods which were once so characteristic of British hill slopes. Today this is a valuable relict habitat, for most similar woods have been cleared and planted with conifers. Near the start of the path is an area which has been replanted with hardwoods under a nursery crop of conifers and a stand of tall beeches has been left by the entrance to demonstrate the fine nature of the original woods.

Lower down, the path runs through the old mixed wood of oak, ash, lime

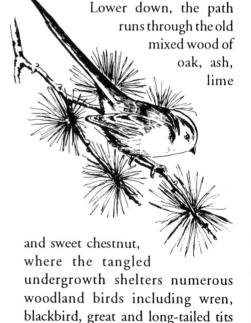

and sweet chestnut, where the tangled undergrowth shelters numerous woodland birds including wren, blackbird, great and long-tailed tits and goldcrest.

7. Keep straight along the Dyke footpath following signposts.

Here the dyke is well-marked as a steep embankment on your left and at one point a seat of stones is recessed into the earthwork. The quartz pebbles in the rock indicate its origin as a beach in Carboniferous times.

8. At the junction of footpaths leave the Dyke path and turn left to follow a track uphill and continue to an open space near an old quarry.

This was the main entrance into the woods and takes you to two buildings on the right which were originally the keeper's cottage and the kennels.

9. For the shorter Route, after reaching the old quarry, turn right and follow a wide cart track down to the lane. Go through a gate into the lane and turn left to walk along it.

This sheltered, sunny lane along a south facing slope is a joy in spring, when all the wild flowers, celandines and moschatel, primroses and violets come out early. The hedgebank just below Llanforda park is known for the abundance of two rare species, spring figwort and evergreen alkanet. According to local tradition they were planted there by Edward Llwyd, the great scholar of the Lloyd family. There can be little doubt that they originally came from the Llanforda garden, for the two were a favourite

combination of the Keeper of the Chelsea Physic Garden, who was employed to design Llanforda garden. They probably escaped three centuries ago, since when they have held their own in competition with the native weeds, so must by now be considered established aliens.

At the road junction turn left and follow the road to the next turn (3). Now turn right into Broomhall Lane and proceed back to Castle View.

To continue by the longer route just beyond the buildings go through a gate and turn right into a field and join a track. Turn left at the quarry continue down the track. Follow the track the full length of the field to a stone wall with a stile.

This field is part of the extensive parkland of Llanforda Hall, where single trees stand out amongst the pasture. Today many of the trees bear great tangles of twigs known as witches brooms. These freak growths can be caused by a fungus or virus which stimulates normally dormant buds into growth.

10. Cross the stile and head towards the wood to a second stile. Beyond this you enter a wooded area.

This area is the tangled remains of the garden of Llanforda Hall, the home of Edward Lloyd who built the Coach and Dogs you saw at the start of your

17

walk. The hall was demolished less than fifty years ago, which shows how quickly thickets can obscure derelict buildings.

11. Follow the footpath to the right through the scrub to reach another stile. This brings you into more parkland, through which a track leads to the road.

12. Now go through the gate, turn left along the road and at the first junction turn right into Broomhall Lane, to reverse your outward route back to Castle View.

# Brogyntyn Hall

OS Map 1:500,000 Sheet No. 126, OS Map 1:25,000 Sheet No. SJ23/33
Distance: 6 miles or 5½ miles

*A walk through the middle of glorious Brogyntyn Park,
taking in the lodge, the hall, the castle and the farm.*

1. The walk starts at Castle View where car parking is available. Walk down Arthur Street and turn right into Willow Street. Continue across the cross roads to the top of Willow Street where five roads meet. Take the one immediately to the right of the Fire Station, which is Oakhurst Road.

Arthur Street was one of the old shuts of the town, where a gate at the bottom could shut off the houses from the cart traffic up Willow Street. A room over the gateway was the meeting place for the first non-conformist services to be held in town.

No 55 Willow Street on your left, was the birthplace of Sir Walford Davies, a chorister and organist of Christ Church, who later became a popular broadcaster and Master of the King's Music.

The crossroads was the site of the Willow, or Welsh Gate through the town walls, and beyond it the road widens as it climbs west to the hills.

On the left a fine Victorian terrace of listed houses, built in 1840, is called Porkington Terrace, which is the old name for Brogyntyn. The stone wall round the Fire Station marks the

Arthur Street

19

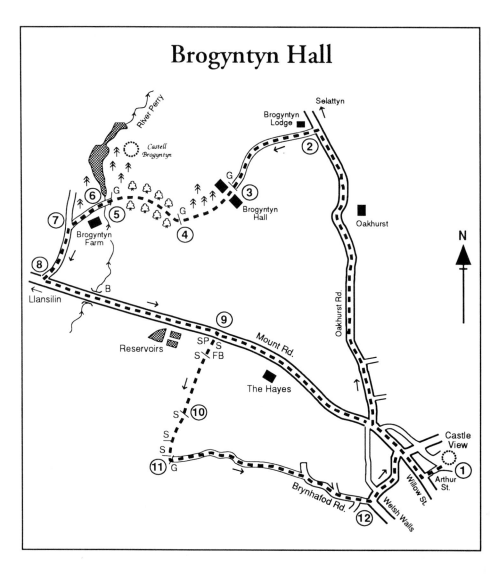

boundary where the Brogyntyn Estate, seat of Lord Harlech, adjoined the town.

Oakhurst, about a mile from town, has fine views towards the Bronze Age earthworks of Old Oswestry. Although constructed only about one hundred and fifty years ago for R. J. Venables, Director of the Great Western and Cambrian railways, it was built in the Elizabethan style of architecture and was at one time known as Mount Zion. In the hedgerow opposite, a mass of winter heliotrope, unusual in the wild in

Britain, has obviously escaped from the Victorian garden.

2. Past Oakhurst, take care as the road is busy and there is no footpath. The first opening in the stone wall to your left is the drive to Brogyntyn, with the old lodge beside it. Follow the drive up to the hall.

As you walk through extensive parkland, you have the opportunity to admire the elegant facade of Brogyntyn Hall which was built in 1730 with alterations made in 1811 by Margaret Ormsby "upon the chaste and pure Grecian style" as then described. The hall was the residence of Lord Harlech until 1957 and afterwards used for some time by British Telecom.

3. Go through the gate by the second cattle grid and follow the path between the hall to the left and stables to the right.

The approach to the stable yard involves a sharp turn through the archway, but reputedly the coachmen prided themselves on negotiating this at full speed.

4. Continue until a gate is reached. Beyond this follow the path to the right through an avenue of lime trees.

On your left is the site of the old icehouse where meat and game were stored in ice through the winter in the Victorian counterpart of the modern refrigerator.

5. The path leaves the boundary of the field.

On your right is a shrubbery round the lake constructed on the upper reaches of the Perry. In the shrubbery a mound marks the site of Castell Brogyntyn the stronghold of Owain, natural son of Madoc ap Meredydd the builder of Oswestry castle.

On your left is the old dairy of the hall.

Brogyntyn Lodge

21

6. Cross through a gate and continue up a slight hill and through Brogyntyn Home Farm to reach a road.

7. Turn left along the road and continue to the crossroads.

8. Turn left into Mount Road and continue past a group of three reservoirs to the pumping station.

Now the road is downhill all the way with extensive views across the Shropshire Plain to Grinshill on the left, Nesscliffe Hill in the foreground, the Wrekin behind, and the Breidden and Long Mountain to the right. The bridge, soon after your turn into the road crosses the infant River Perry.

The reservoirs store Oswestry's supply of soft Welsh water from Pen-y-gwely. With the more recent increase in demand, the supply is now supplemented with harder water from local bore-holes.

9. For the shorter route continue down Mount Road to the junction with Oakhurst Road and retrace your steps to the town centre.

In the wall on your left along Mount Road look for an old boundary stone inscribed, S.P.O.R. standing for Selattyn Parish and Oswestry Rural.

Opposite the stone is a thick shrubbery surrounding The Hayes. This ancient cruciform house is reputed to be the oldest house in Oswestry and is thought to have originally been a monastery. It is also said to be still haunted by a transgressing monk.

For the longer route, turn right off Mount Road just before the pumping station and cross a stile to join a footpath which leads to a stile then crosses two small footbridges. Cross the next stile and follow the line of the field.

10. Cross a stile in the corner and continue the line across another stile.

11. After crossing a stile in the corner of the field go left through a nearby gate into a grassy track which leads into Brynhafod Lane and then Brynhafod Road.

Although this lane provides a shady alternative to the main road, it is usually damp so the grass is lush and the lower end, muddy at the best of times, can become a stream after heavy rain.

A little before the present limit of the houses, the land was formerly crossed by an ancient trackway from The Hayes in Mount Road to Strata Marcella Abbey near Welshpool.

12. Turn left into Welsh Walls.

The amount of stone incorporated into the buildings here is an indication of the recycling of a valuable resource as the town walls, which ran along this road, fell into disuse.

**13.** Turn right into Willow Street, then left up Arthur Street to return to Castle View.

# Morda Valley

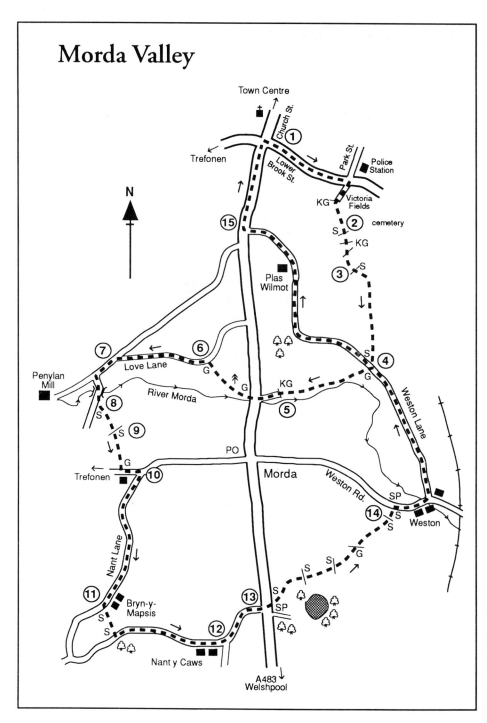

# Morda Valley

OS Map 1:50,000 Sheet No 126, OS Map 1:25,000 Sheet No. SJ22/32
Distance: 6½ miles

*A walk through the valley of the
River Morda learning about its industial past.*

1. From the traffic lights go down Lower Brook Street as far as the Police Station. Just opposite take the road through the new housing estate of Victoria Fields following it round to the right to a kissing gate into a field.

2. Follow the field path over the stile by the corner of the cemetery and then through the two kissing gates.

3. Cross a stile into a narrow tree-lined path and follow this round to the right.

4. Cross the stile at the end into Weston Lane and turn right. Almost immediately on your left go through a gate to follow the footpath which keeps near the right hedge. When the hedge changes direction, cross to the other side of the field where the Morda Brook is on your left.

5. Go through the kissing gate into a lane and turn right to reach the main road. Go straight across the road and through the gate by the cattle grid. Follow the path parallel with the brook and continue past the orchard on the right.

Morda was a busy industrial centre during the last century, with coal mines and mills. As you leave the field path to enter a lane, a building on your left, now a car repair workshop was formerly a cotton mill. The Morda Brook which drove it also turned a corn mill beside the main road on the other side of the road bridge.

6. Cross over the gate and turn left into Love Lane.

7. Turn left and follow the lane round to the left.

As the lane turns sharply to the left, the drive straight ahead is the entrance to another old corn mill, called Pen-y-lan. Its tall brick chimney, built for the conversion from water to steam power, can still be seen, but competition from cheap imported wheat, milled near the ports, made Pen-y-lan unviable before the conversion was made.

8. Cross the bridge, then climb the first stile on the left and walk diagonally across the field to the far hedgerow.

9. Climb the steps, cross the stile and continue across the next field.

10. Go through the gate, turn left along the road, then in a short distance turn right into Nant Lane.

The building on the corner of the lane was originally an inn, in which the share out of the week's wages to miners of the Drill Colliery was made on Saturdays, and its name The Hen and Chickens, is still retained.

11. After passing the farm of Bryn-y-mapsis, cross the stile on the left side and follow the edge of the field. Cross the stile into the lane and turn left.

This lane runs along Nant-y-caws, the deeply cut valley of a small stream. The south-facing bank of its left slope is bright with both wild and garden flowers in spring, while beyond the brook is the Rough, an old mining area which later became scrubland, with gorse and brambles, before being reclaimed to good pasture in recent years.

12. At the junction with the Sweeney Mountain road turn left.

13. At the main Welshpool road, cross to the other side and over a stile to reach a footpath across the field, keeping just to the left of a small copse.

Your path takes you past a steep-sided artificial pool, which is in fact the clay-pit that supplied the Sweeney brickworks attached to Sweeney coal-mine. The clay was so suitable for the work that large consignments of blue bricks were exported as far as Holland.

14. Follow the footpath across a series of stiles until Weston Road is reached. Turn right into Weston Road then left into Weston Lane

Pen-y-lan

Weston Mill

which will take you back to Oswestry.

The hamlet of Weston grew into a busy community with the coming of the railway which crosses the Morda Brook here. A wharf was built to receive the produce of the many mills along its course for rail transport further afield. The tall building near the road junction is Weston Mill which is still operative as a bakery, and although electricity is now the driving force, it is still possible to switch back to water power in an emergency.

Where Weston Lane takes a sharp turn to the right, a gate on your left leads into an old linear wood of mixed trees which is scheduled to be preserved as a nature reserve.

As you near the town, the first large house on the left is Plas Wilmot, the birthplace of Wilfred Owen, the well-known soldier poet who was killed in battle only days before the 1918 armistice.

15. At the T-Junction, where your lane meets Morda Road, turn right and continue straight on past the traffic lights into Church Street and the centre of town.

The house on the left of the junction is the gatehouse of the toll-gate which spanned the road here in the last century to collect payment for the use of the road from travellers passing through.

# Trefonen

Castle View

Arthur St.

(1)

The Cross

Church St.

Trefonen

(2)

↑
(17)

Upper Church St.

Penylan Lane

(3)

B

Penylan Mill

SP S

S

↑ Oswestry

(5)

S SP

(4)

(16)

Morda

S

Gwerni

S

(6)

S

PH

Sch

(7)

Brook House

PH

(8)

S

(9)

Trefonen

Pentre Farm

Woodhill

S S S

(12)

(13)

S

SP

(10)

S S

S

(11)

S

(15)

G

(14)

N

↓
Treflach

28

# Trefonen

OS Map 1:50,000 Sheet No 126, OS Map 1:25,000 Sheet No. SJ 22/32
Distance: 7 miles

*A walk along lanes and through pasture
to the village of Trefonen to learn of the area's mining past.*

1. The walk begins at Castle View where parking is available. Walk down Arthur Street and turn left. At the Cross, turn right into Church Street and continue straight across the traffic lights into Upper Church Street.

This area was previously known as Pentre-poeth or the burnt end of town because of the destructive fires which occurred during the border conflict between the Welsh and English.

2. Take the first turn right into Penylan Lane.

As you walk the lane, the first field on your right is the scene of the Battle of Oswestry in 642 AD in which the Christian King Oswald was killed and impaled. Pilgrims, who came to pray for his soul in the monastery built near the site of the present St Oswald's Church, liked to carry back a small bag of the soil from the spot where he fell. This was reputed to have miraculous healing and protective qualities and was so prized that the hole dug at the sacred spot is said to have been deeper than the height of a man, and the monastery flourished remarkably on the alms given.

3. At the T-junction, cross over the stile directly ahead. Follow the line of the stream to the left for some way, then cross diagonally to your right to cross a stile and follow the hedge.

As your lane, narrow and rural after the rear entrance to Pen-y-llan, climbs the bank on the far side of the bridge over the Morda, it joins Chain Lane. This got its name from the chain put across, where travellers were stopped and charged a toll, so foiling attempts to avoid the toll-gate on the main road by using by-ways.

In the field by the stream the mounds are old spoil heaps, for this was the site of the New British Gate Pit sunk in 1861, and the cottages by the next hedge were colliery offices.

4. Cross over the stile and turn right

along the road as far as Eunant Cottages on your right.

The three stone cottages at the far end were contemporaneous with the pit, and comprised the Tommy shop, butcher's and tap room to supply the miners in a region remote from the shops.

5. Opposite the cottages, cross the stile and follow the hedge on your left. Cross the next stile in front of the farmhouse, continue beside the buildings, then follow the line of the hedge. Where this turns off to the left, continue straight across the field.

6. Cross the stile, then the next one opposite and afterwards keep alongside the hedge on your right.

7. Cross the stile in the right-hand corner of the field into a path between a house and the fields. This path leads into a road which takes you past the school to the main road.

8. This is the centre of Trefonen, with the Barley Mow across the road to the right and the Efel Inn to the left. Take road opposite and go past Efel Inn.

The Efel Inn was an important place a century ago, for it was here that the chalters (from "chaldron" - a measure of coal) would pay out the miners' wages. In each pit, the chalter would receive the due amount for the quantity of coal extracted during the week and on Saturday evening he would distribute to each collier his due. That the amount seemed a small enough return for a week of hard work is suggested by the nicknames given to the two chalter rooms at the Efel, which were, "The Rogues Hole" and "The Devil's Nook". Wives usually queued here too, to collect their housekeeping money before too much of the wage found its way back into mine host's till.

9. After a short distance, cross the stile on your left and follow the footpath down to the main road. Cross over this road, and a stile will lead you into a small field. The footpath then leads to the hedge on your

right, where you will cross another stile to a footbridge over a small stream. Cross stile on the opposite bank and the footpath veers to the left to the next stile, which is visible in the hedgerow. Cross this, and continue over the next stile.

10. Walk diagonally uphill and climb over the stile. Cut the corner of the field and head for the far edge of the wood on your left. Follow the edge of the field past Pentre Farm.

11. Cross the stile and follow the line of the outbuildings and the field to the left. Cross the next stile.

12. Walk to the left of the lip of high ground and cross over the stile. Continue by following the fence off to the left.

13. At the corner of the field go straight on over the stile with a wooded area to the right. Cross over the stile and follow the footpath across the next field.

14. Cross the gate in the far corner of the field and turn left on to the road. Continue on the road round to the left, following the sign to Oswestry.

15. At the next junction, take the turning to the left.

Soon on the left you will see some fine beech, oak and horse chestnut trees which stand in the parkland of Woodhill. Formerly this was the residence of John Dumville Lees a benefactor of the Trefonen and Treflach areas where the geological boundary between limestone and coal resulted in many quarries and pits. For the workers in these, he built the Cocoa Rooms in Treflach where workers could eat their lunch with a hot drink rather than face the temptations of the "Demon Drink" in a local pub.

Just below Woodhill, Brookhouse, now an old peoples' home, has a picturesque setting by the little stream which, lower down, flows through Nant-y-caws.

Half a mile on the right, yet another coal shaft can be identified in a birch wood standing on a large mound. When felling in Bwlytai Wood, by Pentre Farm, drove the birds from an extensive rookery, they built new nests in this birch wood. In only a few years they abandoned them, perhaps sensing that the foundations into an old mineshaft do not meet the rooks' impeccable safety standards.

16. At the T-junction with the main road, turn right and then immediately left.

17. Follow this lane downhill to the bridge over the Morda, then uphill through the town's surburb into Morda Road. Here, turn left to come into Upper Church Street and so retrace your route to Castle View.

31

Just before you turn into Morda Road, you will find the Croeswylan Stone embedded into the Wall of The Marches School. This stone is the base of The Cross of Weeping set up outside the limits of the town during the great plague of 1559. Fearful of catching this dreaded disease, the countryfolk brought their produce only to the town's outskirts, receiving payment in coins immersed in water and vinegar at the base of the cross.

# Old Racecourse

OS Map 1:50,000 Sheet No. 126, OS Map 1:25,000 Sheet No. SJ23/33
Distance: 8½ miles

*A walk through fields and woods, up onto the
Old Racecourse which offers spectacular views of the surrounding hills.*

1. The walk starts at Castle View where car parking is available. Walk down Arthur Street and turn right into Willow Street. Continue over the crossroads, then bear right at the Fire Station into Oakhurst Road. Continue up Oakhurst Road past Oakhurst Stables on the right and Brogyntyn Lodge on the left. The road is busy here at times, so please take care.

2. Take the next lane on the left, signposted to Pant Glas.

The first farm on your left was unique, early this Century, in that practically all the animals and birds were white, a response to the wish of the owner, Lady Harlech.

A little further on, a wide stone bridge over the lane carries a track from Brogyntyn Hall to the lodge on the Weston Rhyn road. When we were young, going through this tunnel was a frightening challenge taken at a run with handkerchiefs over our heads. A large colony of bats roosted there and awakened by our creams would fly low over our heads, causing great alarm lest they become inextricably entangled in our hair as the old folk forecast. Today we know that, guided by an amazingly accurate echo

Pant Glas

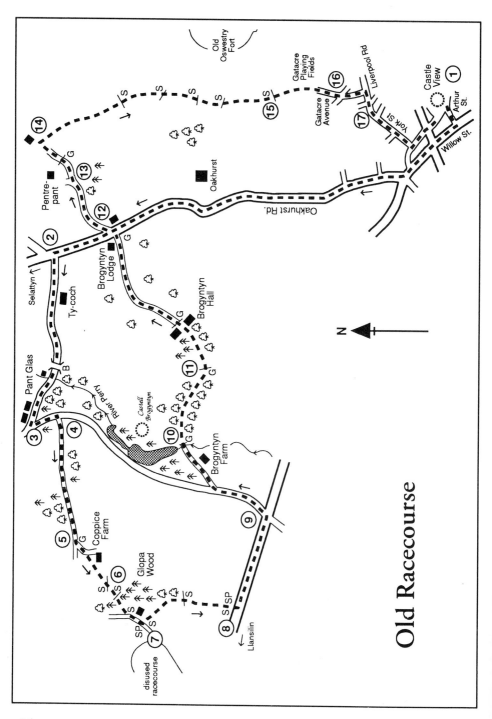

# Old Racecourse

sounding device, they would do no such thing; and we would happily welcome back this colony which, like so many others, has long since succumbed to the improved farming methods using insecticides, which have deprived them of their food.

The lane continues past some fine beech trees, into the tidy hamlet of Pant Glas, built to accommodate the workers on the Brogyntyn Estate.

3. At the road junction, turn left and follow the lane uphill.

4. Take the first turn right up Brummagem Bank and past the old kennels. Soon the surface deteriorates till the lane becomes a track bordered by woodlands.

Some old trees were felled here in the early 1930's and under the bark was discovered a timber beetle so rare that it is now housed in the Natural History Museum in Kensington.

5. At Coppice Farm, on your left, turn through the gate and follow the farm drive for a short distance. At the end of the line of trees, follow the footpath off to the right. Cross through the stile and continue in the same direction across the next field.

6. Cross over the stile into Glopa Wood, follow the path through to the other side, then climb over the stile into a sandy lane. Follow this to

the left past a house with some peacocks.

You are now over 1,000 ft above sea level on the ridge of a millstone grit which forms The Racecourse. It is surprising to realise that during the Great Ice Age, the pressure of ice moving down from the north was sufficient to push ice from the Irish Sea up over this area. On melting, this ice deposited its load of sea sand, which was later extracted from a sand hole a hundred yards to your right by Liverpool Waterworks for its filter beds at Oswestry. The finding of sea shells in the sand confirms its Irish Sea origin.

7. Cross over a stile on the left and follow the footpath to the wood. Join the edge of the wood and follow the footpath to the stile. Continue to the second stile and then follow the edge of the field to the road.

8. Cross the stile and turn left down Mount Road.

9. At the next crossroads turn left into Whitewell Lane, then soon turn right into Brogyntyn Home Farm. Go through the farmyard and continue through a wooded area by a stream which is the infant River Perry.

10. Cross over the gate and follow the avenue of lime trees to the second gate.

11. Beyond this gate continue along the track passing between the stables and Brogyntyn Hall. Cross through the gate to the right of the cattle grid and continue down the drive to the lodge.

Brogyntyn Hall, the former residence of the Lords Harlech was restored in 1811 by Margaret Ormsby in the Grecian style. On the pediment of the portico, the arms of the Ormsby Gores may be seen in high relief.

12. Here a gate by another cattle grid takes you into Oakhurst Road. Cross the road and almost immediately opposite enter the drive to Pentre Pant.

13. Leave the drive to follow the track branching to the right, and go through the gate by the cattle grid. Avoid the footpath leading off to the left and continue straight on.

14. The footpath cuts right, across the field towards an old hedge, now just a line of tall bushes. Now climb to the skyline keeping the hedge to your left, cross the stile and continue in the same direction with Old Oswestry to your left. The path leads over three stiles through two more fields before reaching the field immediately behind the Old Oswestry car park.

15. Now keep to the perimeter of the field to a stile which takes you into a narrow path leading down to the Gatacre Playing Field car park, and so into Gatacre Avenue.

16. Continue down Gatacre Avenue, then along Gatacre Road past the allotments and turn right into Liverpool Road.

Liverpool Road gets its name, as does Vyrnwy Road further to your right, from the fact that the large pipes carrying Liverpool's water supply

Brogyntyn Hall

from Lake Vyrnwy run underground along this route.

17. Liverpool Road runs into York Street which you should follow to the end, then turn left into Oak Street. At the crossroads, cross over Castle Street into Chapel Street and so return to Castle View.

# EXPLORING SHROPSHIRE
with
## *Shropshire Books*

A good walk is much more than satisfying physical exercise. So what is the secret? Local knowledge and even passion - making sure you do not miss the little things of interest along the way - like taking a walk with a good friend, who can chat about the history or the legends, the landscape and the buildings, as you go.

SHROPSHIRE BOOKS have commissioned writers who love the county to write about some of their favourite walks. The whole series is a marvellous introduction to the landscape and the towns of this lovely county.

Gordon Dickins, who wrote 'An Illustrated Literary Guide to Shropshire' and who has introduced television viewers to the county's literary landscape, takes you in the footsteps of his favourite authors in 'Walks with Writers'. Search with him for the scenes which inspired Housman's 'Shropshire Lad' or Walter Scott's 'The Betrothed'.

The Town Trails of Bridgnorth, Ludlow and Much Wenlock unlock the secrets of these historic places. "Few towns have so much to offer for anyone interested in history" wrote Barrie Trinder about Bridgnorth, as a prelude to the exploration of its medieval castle, Victorian shop fronts, promenade, steam railway and river port.

From rivers to canals and Thomas Telford, the great engineer - with walks leaflet No.8 Market Drayton to hand, follow the Shropshire Union Canal, where Telford threw down the gauntlet to the railways with his revolutionary cut-and-fill technique. For breathtaking views and routes to take full advantage of the beautiful scenery, look out for 'A Walking Guide to the Stiperstones', No.6 in the series of walks leaflets.

# BOOKS

**UNDISCOVERED SHROPSHIRE**
14 Walks in North Shropshire
by Eve Powell

**WALKS WITH WRITERS**
by Gordon Dickins and Gladys Mary Coles

**GREEN WALKS FROM OSWESTRY**
by Mary Hignett

## LEAFLETS

**Available Now**

Bayston Hill
Old Racecourse, Oswestry
Bridgnorth
Stiperstones
Ludlow
Stokesay
Market Drayton
Alveley

**Forthcoming**

Acton Scott

## TOWN TRAILS

**Available Now**

Bridgnorth

**Forthcoming**

Ludlow
Much Wenlock

## CYCLE TRAIL

**Available Now**

Corvedale

*For further details of these and many more books on Shropshire contact:*

**SHROPSHIRE BOOKS**
Winston Churchill Building
Radbrook Centre
SHREWSBURY   SY3 9BJ
Telephone: 0743 254043